I0499991

The Supreme Court:
Politics, Power, and Law (Part I)

Newbury Publishing, LLC.

Copyright © 2023 **Newbury Publishing, LLC.**

All rights reserved. Except as permitted under the U.S.
Copyright Act of 1976, no part of this publication may
be reproduced, distributed, or transmitted in any form or by
any means, or stored in a database or retrieval system,
without the prior written permission of the publisher.

If you would like to use material from the book (other
than for review purposes), prior written permission
must be obtained by contacting the publisher
at permission@newburypub.com
Thank you for your support of the author's rights.

Newbury Publishing, LLC
867 Boylston Street, 5th Floor, PMB 203, Boston, MA 02116

Visit our website at www.newburypub.com

The publisher is not responsible for websites (or their
content) that are not owned by the publisher.

Cover and book design by Newbury Publishing, LLC.

The Newbury Publishing name and logo are trademarks
of Newbury Publishing, LLC. All rights reserved.

First eBook Edition September 2023

CONTENTS

INTRODUCTION
The Least Dangerous Branch

As the highest court in what has become the world's most powerful nation, The Supreme Court of the United States sits at the faultline between the ideal and the real, between justice and power, between the serene majesty of The Law and the sometimes bombastic, sometimes grubby disputes that define our politics.

In the arguments before the court, principles clash with ambition and avarice, and it can be difficult to tell which is which. The decisions that the justices hand back are often wise and reasonable, but there have been moments of folly as well, and on more than one occasion it has taken decades for Americans to recognize the difference.

The Constitution of the United States created a federal government with three separate centers of power. First there was the Congress which wrote laws. Then there was the Presidency, which enforced laws and directed the nation's military and diplomacy. Finally there were the federal courts, with the Supreme Court at the peak, which tried cases and interpreted the laws when their meaning was in dispute.

Alexander Hamilton, one of the most respected drafters of the Constitution, would go on to write in *The Federalist Papers* that "the judiciary, from the nature of its functions, will always be the least dangerous to the political rights of the Constitution." He went on to explain that this was because the President would continue to command the armed forces and law enforcement, while the legislature would direct spending and could redraft laws if it were dissatisfied with the court's decisions. The Courts themselves would have few resources of their own -- they would need the cooperation of the chief executive to enforce any of its orders.

But "least dangerous" is not the same as "perfectly safe ."The drafters of the Constitution meant to create a democratic republic, and a democratic republic operates according to laws, with the courts serving as the final arbiter of what the law requires and how it applies in the cases that come up before them. For the American system to work, the courts would need to gain the public's trust, and then they would need to resist the temptation to abuse that trust.

The Supreme Court might not command the military or control the spending, and in that purely material sense it might be the weakest part of the government, but that doesn't mean it isn't essential to the functioning of the whole thing. A weak and indecisive court would invite anarchy. But an overbearing court can create its own injustices.

In theory, a judge should be able to review the statutes and prior decisions and arrive at a judgment based solely on preexisting law. In practice, legislatures are often vague, and cases involve new technologies and social changes that nobody has anticipated. Sometimes a judge cannot avoid falling back on his or her personal preferences. But they must at least consider the problem in legal terms first. And if that fails, a judge should at least try to hand down a decision that will give clear guidance to the next judge who has to deal with a similar case.

By definition the justices of the Supreme Court are left to handle the hardest cases, the most contentious issues where parties and outside observers are least likely to be satisfied and where statutes and precedents give the least guidance. It is a role that calls for the highest levels of intelligence and wisdom, but also a healthy dose of humility.

So a lot depends on the men and women who serve on the court. You might want a judge to be a disciplined legal thinker, but the best are still human beings. As the controversial attorney Roy Cohn put it: "I don't want to know what the law is, I want to know who the judge is." As the Supreme Court's influence has grown, more energy has been put into deciding who the judges will be. Wise as they might be, it is unrealistic to expect the justices of the Supreme Court to resolve every difficult issue themselves. Having the bitter debates over economics, sex, and race turned over to the high court has not made the strife disappear. It has simply transferred the contentiousness over to the process of deciding who the judges will be.

But we cannot realistically hope to make the Supreme Court safe and boring. As French philosopher Alexis de Tocqueville observed way back in the early 1800s: "There is hardly a political question in the United States which does not sooner or later become a judicial one." And that is to be expected. A democratic republic runs on laws that courts must interpret and apply.

As Justice Marshall would point out in the critical early case of *Marbury v. Madison*: "It is emphatically the province and duty of the Judicial Department to say what the law is." The simple process of interpreting existing law -- let alone deciding what the law ought to be -- inevitably makes the Supreme Court an important actor in American history.

One might hope that the courts would merely serve as referees in the never-ending contests between Congress and the President, between the states and the federal government, and between the multitudes of interests. But one shouldn't be so naive as to think that all referees will call the contests precisely the same, or that the referees, no matter how honest, won't affect the game's outcome. Judging is hard but necessary work. The Supreme Court cannot avoid being the scene of political battles. But it is at its best when it manages to rise above them.

CHAPTER ONE
To Say What The Law Is

The new Constitution had decreed that there should be a Supreme Court but said nothing more about how it would function or where it would sit, or even how many justices there would be. It was up to Congress to fill in a lot of the gaps. The Judiciary Act of 1789 created federal trial courts -- the Supreme Court would primarily serve to hear appeals from them   and set the number of justices on the Supreme Court at six.

President George Washington quickly chose six men to serve. They were all solid legal scholars and reliable Federalists, committed to cementing the authority of the new national government.

In the early days the biggest challenges facing the Supreme Court were more physical than intellectual. The court lacked a dedicated courtroom or offices for research and writing. The Supreme Court's sessions were held in whatever courtroom the justices could find in New York and Philadelphia as the national Capitol moved around.

It wasn't until 1810 that the court had a permanent home, an improvised courtroom built in what was originally the meeting room of the US Senate. It was a cramped space, not much larger than a typical living room today. There was little room for clerks. The court held oral arguments in this little courtroom, but the justices did most of the rest of their work at home -- looking up cases at their home libraries.

But the real challenge came from "riding circuit" -- Supreme Court justices were expected to serve as judges on federal courts, riding from courthouse to courthouse out in the hinterlands hearing cases. This meant leaving home for months at a time and taking stagecoaches over rough roads throughout the states. Traveling over land was arduous at the time. The fastest horse-drawn carriage couldn't go much faster than a person on foot -- about three or four miles an hour. Roads were even rougher out west, where new states like Kentucky and Ohio were being added to the Union -- and to the circuits that the Supreme court justices needed to travel through.

Back home in Washington, the court mostly kept its head down. Over the first decade the court handled fewer than 90 cases, and court reporters of the period show that the court issued opinions on only half of these. During the administration of John Adams Congress passed a series of very controversial laws known as the Alien and Sedition Acts meant to limit criticism of the government. These laws clashed with the First Amendment's protection of free speech, but for whatever reason there was never an appeal to the Supreme Court.

John Jay was the first Chief Justice of the Supreme Court. He was born to a wealthy family of merchants in New York City and was a leader in the Revolution. He was considered an excellent jurist, but he would make his mark as a diplomat. While serving as Chief Justice, he could still negotiate an important treaty with Great Britain. Shortly after that, he left the court and was elected Governor of New York.

The one time that the Supreme Court did manage to make a controversial decision, it was knocked down in no uncertain terms. In *Chisholm v. Georgia*, decided in 1793, the court allowed a South Carolinian to proceed with a debt-collection suit against the State of Georgia. State officials howled in protest -- state governments, the argued, should not be sued in the federal court system. Congress responded by proposing the 11th Amendment, which barred such lawsuits. The states ratified the amendment quickly, negating the *Chisholm* decision. In the future private citizens who wanted to sue a state would need to go through that state's court system -- though clever lawyers would find workarounds.

After Jay left he was briefly replaced by Oliver Ellsworth, a successful attorney from Connecticut who had served in the Senate and had a hand in drafting the Judiciary Act. Like Jay, Ellsworth would finish his term as Chief Justice with a stint as a diplomat, patching up relations with revolutionary France, before retiring from public service in 1800.

The Supreme Court's initial "safe and boring" phase would end when John Adams appointed John Marshall Chief Justice. Marshall hailed from Germantown Virginia, about 60 miles west of the Capital, where his father had a plantation. Young Marshall had little in the way of formal education, but he was an avid reader, and among the books he read was Blackstone's Commentaries on the Laws of England -- the premier guide to British Common Law at the time. During the War for Independence he joined a Virginia regiment and rose to the rank of Lieutenant.

Marshall studied law at the College of William and Mary, John Marshall served in the Virginia Legislature and developed his law practice. He was well respected as an attorney, and argued in front of the US Supreme Court in favor of a Virginia law claiming debts owed to British subjects after the Revolution. Marshall's performance won him respect for his legal skills, although his client ultimately lost the case.

John Marshall was then tapped to serve on a delegation to France. The delegation was told they would need to pay a bribe before they would be allowed to meet with key French officials. They refused and returned to the United States. The incident led to friction between the allies for a while, but Marshall was not blamed. Instead he was appointed Secretary of State for the last few years of the Adams administration. After that, Adams appointed John Marshall to the Supreme Court to replace Chief Justice Ellsworth.

In his last few days as Secretary of State, Marshall would neglect to forward a judicial commission to one William Marbury, an oversight that was to have significant ramifications for John Marshall and the Supreme Court as a whole.

Marshall was not known as a great legal scholar, but he was a strong debater with a knack for persuading others. Any shortcomings he might have had as a legal theorist were made up for by his strong sense of justice and his ability to recognize the central issue in a case.

Chief Justice Marshall sought to build camaraderie among the six court members, and have the court present a more united front.

In the past, Supreme Court Justices would each give their own opinions on every case verbally -- a process that could lead to confusion. Even if court observers were able to take good notes there were bound to be differences between judges for lawyers to pounce upon. Under Marshall the court began to issue a single majority ruling that individual judges would sign on to.

Just as important, Marshall convinced his associate judges to share a single rooming house with him when they were in Washington to hear arguments. Working and living together gave the Justices time to sharpen their arguments, work out their differences, and build a sense of camaraderie. Much of the culture of the court today has its roots in the Supreme Court that John Marshall built.

That new Supreme Court would be put to the test when Mr. Marbury came around for his own judicial posting. The case of *Marbury v. Madison* was filled with political complications.

As the Federalist President John Adams was preparing to leave the Presidency, he appointed many judges, mainly to prevent his successor, the Antifederalist Thomas Jefferson, from filling those same posts. The Secretary of State had the job of formally drafting the notices of appointment ("commissions") and delivering them to the appointees. Before leaving his Secretary of State post, John Marshall had drafted Marbury's commission papers but had not arranged for delivery. When Jefferson's Secretary of State, James Madison, arrived at his office, the commission was still there. Madison held on to the papers. Marbury sued to have them delivered.

As it happened, Marbury filed his suit directly with the Supreme Court. There was a federal statute that allowed for this, but Marshall noticed that the Constitution itself didn't allow for the Supreme Court to take on this particular type of case. What Marshall did with that was, depending on how you look at it, either a straightforward application of law or a dazzling bit of legal and political jiu-jitsu.

In legal terms this was a case of jurisdiction -- which types of cases a court could hear and not hear. William Marbury's complaint asked the Supreme Court to issue what was called a "Writ of Mandamus" -- essentially a command that a public officer take some action -- in this case the writ would go to Secretary of State Madison, and it would command him to deliver Mr. Marbury his commission.

Congress had passed legislation allowing the Supreme Court to issue Writs of Mandamus. But the Constitution had set the Supreme Court up to serve primarily as a court of appeals. And issuing a Writ of Mandamus had always been a job for a trial court.

So, could the Supreme Court give the order or not? To make a long story short, Marshall and his associate judges decided that the Constitution created both the Supreme Court and Congress and spelled out their responsibilities. So the Constitution trumped, the Supreme Court could not hand down a Writ of Mandamus, and Congress could not say otherwise.

If William Marbury had gone to a federal trial court first, and they had refused, he could have appealed to the Supreme Court, which would have been fine. But taking the shortcut cost him his job. The Constitution was the

Supreme Law of the Land, and it was the Supreme Court's responsibility to apply it. And if that meant negating a statute passed by Congress, so be it. It is emphatically the province and duty of the Judicial Department to say what the law is," Marshal concluded. And in this case, ironically, the law was that the Supreme Court could not assist William Marbury.

The law is complicated enough, but the politics made *Marbury v. Madison* so critical. John Marshall and his fellow justices were all Federalists, as were John Adams and William Marbury. Incoming President Thomas Jefferson was an Antifederalist. Marbury was one of the beneficiaries of a series of last-minute appointments that had antifederalists screaming.

At the same time, Jefferson was opposed to a strong Supreme Court that could overturn laws passed by Congress. By passing up on issuing the Writ of Mandamus that William Marbury asked for, the Supreme Court gave Thomas Jefferson a judicial appointment, but at the price of accepting judicial review. And the Supreme Court didn't need any help from Congress or the President to make it stick. Jefferson could have reappointed Marbury -- against his own party's interest -- but it wouldn't have nullified what Marshall had written.

John Marshall took a very controversial step by creating judicial review, but the Supreme Court used it very cautiously. It wouldn't be until after the Civil War that the Supreme Court would strike down another federal statute.

Over the next few years the makeup of the court would change. Associate Justices appointed by the Federalists Washington and Adams retired and Jefferson replaced them with antifederalists. But Marshall remained Chief Justice, and he continued to hold sway. He actually gained an ally when James Madison appointed Joseph Story to the court in 1811. Story hailed from Massachusetts, where he taught at the Harvard Law School. If Marshall had a weakness, it was a shortage of formal legal knowledge. As Marshall's partner, Story would more than make up for that.

Together Marshall and Story would continue to prop up a strong federal government and a strong Supreme Court.

In the 1821 case of *Cohens v. Virginia*, they determined that the Supreme Court could review state court decisions on criminal law. Being prudent, they let the state court's rulings stand, but this stance would prove to be critical later on.

McCulloch v. Maryland was a critical test of federal government authority. As part of its response to an economic downturn, the federal government created The Bank of the United States to manage the country's debt and increase the amount of credit available to investors.

But the bank was also a private company that paid investors dividends, making it controversial. Many states sought to protect their local banks and passed laws to keep the Bank of the United States from operating. Maryland passed a law that forced the bank to pay a $15,000 fee before opening a branch in that state.

Could Maryland get away with that? Was the federal government even allowed to set up a bank? The attorney representing the state argued that the Constitution didn't say Congress could establish a bank. The Bank's lawyers responded that federal laws trumped state laws. And they also said the bank was part of a plan to regulate nationwide commerce, which was in Constitution. The Constitution also gave Congress the power to pass laws "which shall be necessary and proper" for executing its other responsibilities.

Marshall and Story opted for the broader version of Congressional power, allowing the Bank of the United States to operate and striking Maryland's special fee. In ruling as they did, they established that the Constitution would be read broadly, with an eye toward the founders' goal of establishing a strong union. In their view, a pedantic reading that limited the federal government too strictly would defeat the whole purpose of the Constitution.

The decision led to rumblings in many state capitals, especially in the southern states. If federal law was supreme, and federal powers were broad, the risk that the federal government might find a reason to restrict slavery -- or even abolish it outright -- became much greater. "States Rights" became tangled up with the issue of slavery. Eventually slavery would become an issue so divisive that no Supreme Court ruling could settle it.

CHAPTER TWO
That Unfortunate Race

John Marshall passed away in July 1835 after serving 34 years as Chief Justice. President Andrew Jackson chose Roger Brook Taney of Maryland to take his place. Taney came from the elite planter class. He was a devout Roman

Catholic -- Maryland was the one state where Protestants did not dominate society.

Since his older brother was expected to inherit the family estate, Taney pursued a career in law, taking up an apprenticeship with a Maryland judge. (This was the preferred method for legal training at the time.) From there he became involved in politics, eventually joining the emerging Democratic party. Taney served at the highest levels of the federal government, as Attorney General and Secretary of the Treasury.

Taney was a capable judge -- some legal scholars would argue he was among the best to head up the Supreme Court -- but his 28 years as Chief Justice are mostly remembered for one colossal blunder: the case of *Dred Scott v. Sandford*.

African American Slavery was the one great weakness in the American system of government. The drafters of the Constitution had assumed that it would wind itself down over time. Before the war of independence the northern states were in the process of emancipating all the slaves in their territories with an eye toward an eventual ban. The Continental Congress banned slavery in the area northwest of the Ohio River -- modern-day Ohio, Indiana, Illinois, Wisconsin, and Michigan -- before it had even called for the constitutional convention. Even in the southern states many leading figures were ambivalent about the practice.

But the southern states would have balked at an outright ban, so the drafters dodged the issue. There were compromises scattered throughout -- none of these mentioned slavery explicitly, but everyone knew what they were talking about. Congress banned the importation of slaves from Africa in 1808, as soon as the Constitution allowed them to. For the purposes of redistricting states could count 3/5 of their slave population -- the notorious 3/5 compromise. States were obligated to return runaway slaves once they were identified.

By the time Taney took his spot on the court, slavery had been almost entirely abolished from the northern states; only a relative handful of elderly African American slaves remained in the northeast. In the midwest the old Northwest Ordinance and its ban on slavery had held firm. To the extent slaves could be found there they were most likely to be travelers passing through. Dred Scott was one of them.

But the process of abolition stalled there. In the southern states agriculture was dominated by large cotton plantations that had grown dependent on cheap slave labor. The northern states might have freed their own slaves, but northern industry wasn't completely blameless -- northern mills depended on southern cotton.

And northern voters did not expect their representatives to press for emancipation at the federal level. Northern workers were committed to keeping slavery away from their states and towns but were willing to leave slavery undisturbed where it existed.

But conflict over slavery was escalating. The main bone of contention was the spread of slavery into new territories and states. States tended to be admitted in pairs -- one free state and one slave state. The territories became battlegrounds, sometimes literally. The territory of Kansas in effect had two governments -- one pro-slavery, the other anti-slavery -- and rival militias and guerilla bands attacking each other.

In 1836 and 1837 Dred Scott accompanied his master, an Army doctor named John Ellison, on assignments in the state of Illinois and the Wisconsin Territory, both of which were free territories. In 1846 -- now back home in the slave state of Missouri, Scott sued for his freedom. Missouri's State Supreme Court turned him down initially. But Dr. Emerson passed away, and the executor of Emerson's estate was one John Sanford, a resident of New York. Since Sanford and Scott were residents of different states, Dred Scott could sue again, this time in federal court, and take his appeal to the US Supreme Court.

The Union had expanded greatly since the time when Marshall was appointed Chief Justice. The members of the Supreme Court still needed to ride circuits, though the growth of the railroads had made that duty a bit less demanding. With more states added in the west Congress added three circuits and three justices to cover them; the court reached its current membership of nine.

Scott's attorneys argued that their client was entitled to his freedom because he had traveled through parts of the country where slavery was illegal -- the time Emerson and Scott spent in Illinois and the Wisconsin Territory severed the bond between master and slave. The case reached the Supreme Court in 1856. It was hoped that the Supreme Court could work out a settlement on the slavery question.

But the Constitution did not lay out the grounds for a permanent resolution, and Chief Justice Taney was not in a mood to split differences when he sat down to draft the court's decision.

As it was with *Marbury v. Madison*, the decision hinged on jurisdiction -- was Dred Scott a citizen who could sue in federal court? Writing for a majority of seven justices, Taney said no:

> It is difficult at this day to realize the state of public opinion in relation to that unfortunate race which prevailed in the civilized and enlightened portions of the world at the time of the Declaration of Independence and when the Constitution of the United States was framed and adopted. But the public history of every European nation displays it in a manner too plain to be mistaken.

> They had for more than a century before been regarded as beings of an inferior order, and altogether unfit to associate with the white race either in social or political relations, and so far inferior that they had no rights which the white man was bound to respect, and that the negro might justly and lawfully be reduced to slavery for his benefit.

Taney's opinion had drastic implications for the African-American population. By his terms even black freedmen were in a precarious position, because their own liberties came at the sufferance of the white population.

Even by the standards of his own time, looking at the precedents that had been set before *Dred Scott*, Taney was wrong. Federal courts had allowed blacks to sue whites in the past. In the case of *Elkay v. Ives and Moss* a freedman from Massachusetts sued slave traders for the return of his daughters. A jury determined that the girls were taken illegally, ordered them freed, and awarded damages. This happened back in 1793, when the northern states were still in the process of emancipation themselves.

But Taney didn't stop there. He also declared that the federal government did not have the authority to ban slavery in the territories -- where new state governments were being formed.

This decision brought howls of protest from the northern states, where the majority were willing to leave southern plantation owners alone but did not want slavery where they lived. They understandably feared the admission of new slave states. To make matters worse, Taney treated slavery itself as a sort of fundamental right, instead of something that the founders tolerated for the sake of establishing a federal union. Taney's decision, and the reasoning behind it, put anti-slavery laws in the north on shaky ground.

Chief Justice Taney did have one legitimate point: the north's abolition of slavery was motivated more by the interests of the free white population than justice for black slaves. White laborers feared that their wages and status would be undercut if slave labor were an option. Northern states were not always welcoming to black freedmen and were inconsistent about extending voting and other rights.

But the north's failings did not turn slavery into any sort of fundamental right, and Taney's attempt to make it one only hardened northerners' determination to prevent slavery's spread. In time it would be clear that toleration was untenable: preserving the Union would require the eradication of slavery.

The court's own reputation took severe damage. Taney had hoped to find a resolution to the issue of slavery in the Constitution itself. But it wasn't there, and Taney's attempt to tease one out of the text led him to misread the Constitution and erect a moral monstrosity. Later on another Supreme Court Justice, Charles Evans Hughes, would call Dred Scott "a self-inflicted wound."

If there was a silver lining in all this, Dred Scott's owners turned Scott and his family over to a Republican congressman named Taylor Blow shortly after the Supreme Court issued its decision. Blow gave the Scotts their manumission papers a couple of months later. Dred Scott himself was a free man.

Four years later Abraham Lincoln took office as the first President elected from the Republican party, a party committed to halting the spread of slavery -- though not quite ready to advocate outright abolition. As southern states broke away from the Union and formed their Confederacy, one might expect that a Chief Justice who had taken a strong position in favor of slavery would resign or even be impeached.

But Taney remained committed to the Union, at least in his own mind. His position was incredibly awkward, though. His home state of Maryland allowed slavery and might have joined the Confederacy if its citizens had been given a chance to vote on it. If Maryland had seceded the federal Capitol would have been surrounded by Confederate territory, so Union forces moved in quickly and shut down any secessionist activity there.

It was a near-run thing. The Maryland Legislature voted against secession initially, but the state's Governor, Thomas Holliday Hicks, was determined not to let troop trains in from the north. He called on John Merryman, a state legislator and a Lieutenant in the state militia, to blow up bridges as part of the plan. Union troops arrested Merryman and held him at Fort McHenry.

Merryman petitioned for a Writ of Habeas Corpus. This old English legal process required the government to show up in court with a prisoner and provide the judge with a legal justification for his or her arrest. Habeas Corpus is an essential protection against arbitrary imprisonment, and the Constitution itself guarantees that prisoners have the right to request the writ and the hearing -- except in times of invasion or rebellion.

Which is what was going on in Maryland at the time Merryman was hauled into Fort McHenry. President Lincoln declared that the writ of Habeas Corpus would not be enforced until order was restored.

As it turned out, Roger Taney was assigned to the Maryland circuit, and he issued the Habeas writ for Merryman. Following Lincoln's orders, the commander at For McHenry refused to bring Merryman, sending a junior officer with a message for Taney that Merryman was a suspected saboteur and that Habeas protections were suspended. Taney then wrote a decision on his own authority, stating that only Congress could suspend the enforcement of the Writ of Habeas Corpus.

As a matter of law Taney had a fair point. The Constitutional provision on Habeas was in the section on the powers of Congress, even if it didn't explicitly say who could or couldn't suspend Habeas protections. The clear implication was that only Congress could take this step.

But in political terms Taney himself was close to powerless. Lincoln simply ignored Taney's protests, and with war breaking out he paid no political or legal price for doing so. Congress would retroactively approve Lincoln's actions when it returned to session, and the Supreme Court would not challenge any of Lincoln's policies during the remainder of the Civil War. Merryman would be charged with treason, but was eventually released without being tried.

Taney was also old, and his health was declining. He passed away in 1864, with the war still raging.

CHAPTER THREE
Reconstruction

T he latter half of the 1860s was a time of change for America and the Supreme Court. The most obvious was the court moving to better accommodations. The Capitol

Building was thoroughly renovated during the Civil War, including the construction of its famous dome. The Senate got a new meeting place, and the Supreme Court took over the prior Senate Chambers.

Their new courtroom was larger and more comfortable, offering more seats for observers, a lobby for attorneys, and space for the justices to put on their robes. It did not, however, provide room for offices or a library. Justices would still need to do much of their research and writing at home or at legal libraries around Washington.

The changes were more than cosmetic: the number of justices was set permanently at nine. And most important of all, they got some relief from riding circuit; instead of riding circuit every year, they were given every other year off, which was a good thing because the number of cases coming up for review was climbing steadily.

The Constitution itself was changed dramatically. Three new amendments changed the role of the federal government and the balance of power with the states. The 13th Amendment abolished slavery outright. The Civil War had not started out as a war to end slavery, but over time it evolved into one. Lincoln's Emancipation Proclamation had begun the process. Slaves were set free as Union troops moved through the Confederacy. The 13th Amendment completed it, emancipating the slaves that remained. These were mainly in Missouri, Kentucky, Maryland, and other areas where slavery was practiced but did not rebel.

The 14th Amendment established a standard of national citizenship and established rights to due process and equal protection under the law. This was widely seen as a final rebuke to the Supreme Court's ruling in *Dred Scott v. Sandford*. But over time the Supreme Court would use it for purposes far removed from that. The 14th Amendment would turn out to be the most consequential of the three. Many of its effects would be beneficial. Others would be more dubious.

The 15th Amendment created a right to vote regardless of race, color, or earlier condition of servitude. The supporters of this amendment were mostly sincere about their intent to have African Americans participate fully in state and national politics, but this amendment would be undermined by the stubbornness of southern leaders and the naivete and indifference of those from the north.

While all this was going on the US Army occupied the southern states. There was a process of "Reconstruction" as state governments were reorganized and prepared for readmission into the federal Union. Notably, all three of these "Reconstruction Amendments" included a provision allowing Congress to enforce their terms through legislation. The federal Congress gained power after the war, but it would fall to the Supreme Court to determine just how much.

As Union forces closed in on the Confederate Capitol in Richmond, Virginia, President Lincoln named Salmon P. Chase to serve as Chief Justice. Chase had been the Governor of Ohio, and later on served as Lincoln's Secretary of the Treasury. Chase was known as an ambitious politician and committed foe of slavery but not as a particularly skilled lawyer. He would turn out to be a weak Chief Justice, and effective leadership fell to others.

The obvious pressing issue of Reconstruction was the place of the former slaves in society. Millions of men and women had been set free, but they had little if any money, no homes of their own, and with some rare exceptions no education to speak of. The Reconstruction Amendments envisioned a nation where those slaves (or at least their descendants) would work for their own wages, be protected by the laws, own property, and participate in government. This would require radical change in the south, if not the entire Union.

The leadership of the victorious north took these goals seriously. The desire was there at the outset. The execution would fall far short of what was needed. For their part, the Justices of the Supreme Court failed to anticipate the lengths that southern whites would go to resist the purposes of the Reconstruction Amendments, and balked at taking the strong measures that were needed to make their guarantees effective.

The Chase Court got off to a solid start. They struck down several state "test oath" statutes. These were meant to keep southern sympathizers out of government and the professions. While the goal of keeping former traitors to the Union out of critical positions was understandable, the majority of Supreme Court justices concluded that they were too broad and acted too much like ex post facto laws that punished men and women for acts that they did before the law was passed -- something that the Constitution explicitly prohibited.

The Supreme Court would go back and forth on a critical economic issue. During the Civil War the government issued paper currency that wasn't backed by gold in order to pay for weapons and supplies. This weakened the value of the dollar and creditors protested. Initially the Supreme Court ruled that creditors were not obligated to accept these "greenbacks." This left millions of paper dollars in circulation whose value was suddenly very much up in the air.

The court reversed itself the following year, with a pair of new justices tipping the balance and ruling that greenbacks were valid currency. Chase had overseen the release of the greenbacks as Lincoln's Treasury Secretary, but he voted against them as a Supreme Court Justice both times.

But Salmon Chase would not be around to deal with the critical issues created by the Reconstruction Amendments. He suffered a stroke in 1870, just before the court shifted on fiat money. A second stroke in 1873 proved to be fatal.

It took President Ulysses Grant more than half a year to find a replacement for Chase. After being turned down by at least one candidate and being told that others were unlikely to be confirmed, Grant finally found Morrison Waite. Waite was a native of New England who attended Yale law school, then settled in Toledo Ohio, where he built up a successful legal practice.

As a lawyer he was known for diligence and a calm temper, but he was not a particularly creative or visionary thinker. One reporter described him as standing "at the front rank of second rank lawyers." As Chief Justice he would try to serve more as a manager of the court's business than as an intellectual leader.

The Supreme Court did benefit from Waite's managerial efforts. Its docket of cases was growing rapidly. As the nation grew, more cases were filed in the federal courts, and more appeals to the Supreme Court, which at the point did not have the ability to choose cases. Waite set an example with his own personal work ethic and convinced his associates to turn in their opinions quickly as well for the most part. The Supreme Court at least managed to keep up with its docket.

The quality of its decisions left something to be desired, however. In retrospect the most jarring ruling came in the *Civil Rights Cases*.

Using its authority under the 13th, 14th, and 15th amendments, Congress passed the first Civil Rights law in 1875, guaranteeing blacks access to public accommodations such as railroads, hotels, and theaters. It was a serious attempt to establish racial equality, but there was an intense backlash against it almost immediately -- and not just in the south. President Grant signed the bill but never put much effort into enforcing it, arguing that securing voting rights was a higher priority.

Nonetheless, complaints were filed against five businesses that either refused black customers or relegated them to segregated sections of trains or theaters. These five complaints were brought together in one case for the Supreme Court to consider.

The result was the gutting of the Civil Rights Act of 1875. By an 8-1 margin the court ruled that racial segregation, however difficult or embarrassing it might be for African Americans, was not a form of slavery. And because the defendants were all private businesses, their discrimination did not violate equal protection of the law. Congress, the court found, did not have the power to act against them.

Associate Justice Joseph Bradley of New Jersey wrote the court's decision:

> There were thousands of free colored people in this country before the abolition of slavery, enjoying all the essential rights of life, liberty, and property the same as white citizens; yet no one, at that time, thought that it was any invasion of their personal status as freemen because they were not admitted to all the privileges enjoyed by white citizens, or because they were subjected to discriminations in the enjoyment of accommodations in inns, public conveyances, and places of amusement.

Justice John Marshall Harlan -- named after former Chief Justice John Marshall -- was the lone dissenter. He observed that:

> Constitutional provisions, adopted in the interest of liberty, and for the purpose of securing, through national legislation, if need be, rights inhering in a

state of freedom, and belonging to American citizenship, have been so construed as to defeat the ends the people desired to accomplish, which they attempted to accomplish, and which they supposed they had accomplished by changes in their fundamental law.

Harlan was particularly troubled by discrimination that would affect African Americans as they traveled:

...it would seem that the right of a colored person to use an improved public highway, upon the terms accorded to freemen of other races, is as fundamental in the state of freedom, established in this country, as are any of the rights which my brethren concede to be so far fundamental as to be deemed the essence of civil freedom. 'Personal liberty consists,' says Blackstone, 'in the power of locomotion, of changing situation, or removing one's person to whatever place one's own inclination may direct, without restraint, unless by due course of law.' But of what value is this right of locomotion, if it may be clogged by such burdens as Congress intended by the act of 1875 to remove?

There is room for debate over the Supreme Court's decision in the *Civil Rights Cases*. The 1875 Civil Rights Act dramatically changed the federal government's role. Up to that point even those who supported a strong federal government had assumed that the regulation of local businesses and their day-to-day operations would be left to the states. In addition, the Supreme Court was developing a strong preference for individual liberty in business dealings. It is unfortunate but understandable that the justices would balk at this shift.

And there is a case to be made that President Grant had the correct priorities: that the first need of African Americans was equal treatment by government itself, along with securing the right to vote -- which would give blacks a say in selecting the Governors and Sheriffs and Judges who enforced local laws. The wording of the Reconstruction Amendments would have given Congress a much stronger basis to act. Vexing as private discrimination often was, Reconstruction might have been more effective if Congress had set different priorities when it passed the first civil rights laws.

But Bradley's decision stands out for its naivety. The end of slavery might have made blacks equal to whites as a matter of legal theory; in practical terms racial equality was a long way off. Bradley's claim that freedmen had enjoyed their liberties "the same as white citizens" when they were discriminated against regularly is hard to fathom. The court's failure to recognize the differences in wealth and social standing would have terrible consequences. One cannot expect Supreme Court Justices to have perfect foresight, but Bradley -- and the seven justices who supported him -- should have known better than that.

The Civil Rights Cases were a bad omen for African Americans. Worse would come as Melville Fuller stepped in as Chief Justice.

Fuller was born in Maine and studied law at Harvard; though he didn't stay long enough to gain his legal degree, he did return to Maine, where he continued as a legal clerk. He then moved to Chicago, where he joined a local law firm and got involved in Democratic party politics. When Chief Justice Waite died in 1888, President Grover Cleveland turned to Fuller to take his place.

It was a contentious nomination. The Republicans controlled the Senate and Fuller was a Democrat. To make matters worse he had a mixed record on the Civil War and slavery. Fuller supported the war effort but was critical of Lincoln's direction, and he opposed efforts to eliminate slavery. He did have good relations with Illinois' two Republican Senators, though, and they vouched for his personal character. When the confirmation vote came the Republican caucus split while the Democrats were united in his support, putting Fuller on the Supreme Court with several votes to spare.

As Chief Justice Fuller promoted a sense of camaraderie in the court. He instituted the tradition of having all the justices shake hands before beginning sessions. He was not a particularly strong writer but he could be convincing; he was with the majority close to 99 percent of the time. He was adept at distributing assignments, especially the writing of controversial decisions.

The most notorious case of Fuller's time as Chief Justice would be *Plessy v. Ferguson*. Homer Plessy was what folks in Louisiana called an "Octaroon" -- one-eighth black. He could pass for white but he chose not to one afternoon in June 1892 when he boarded an East Louisiana Railroad train in New Orleans for the trip to Covington, on the other side of Lake Ponchartrain.

Under Louisiana law Plessy should have sat in the colored section of the train but he opted to sit with the whites, in violation of Louisiana's Separate Car Act, which called for "separate but equal" seating for the races. A private detective, tipped off in advance, asked Plessy to move. When Plessy refused, he made the arrest.

The whole thing had been a setup. Plessy, the detective, even the railroad were in on it. The goal was to set up a test case to force the Supreme into stating whether states could force private businesses like the railroad to keep African American passengers separated from whites. All involved hoped to see the law struck down. (The railroad opposed the law because of the hassle created by connecting extra railroad cars or erecting physical barriers.)

Four years later the case reached the Supreme Court. Melville Fuller chose another New-Englander-turned-Midwesterner to write the decision: Henry Billings Brown, who had been born in Massachusetts and made his mark in Detroit, Michigan, practicing admiralty law for shipping companies in the Great Lakes.

Aside from Justice Harlan, who was building his reputation as The Great Dissenter, the court was united behind Brown's decision, allowing the Separate Car Act to stand:

We consider the underlying fallacy of the plaintiff's argument to consist in the assumption that the enforced separation of the two races stamps the colored race with a badge of inferiority. If this be so, it is not by reason of anything found in the act, but solely because the colored race chooses to put that construction on it.

John Marshall Harlan was more skeptical about the Louisiana Legislature's motives:

Everyone knows that the statute in question had its origin in the purpose, not so much to exclude white people from railroad cars occupied by blacks, as to exclude colored people from coaches occupied by or assigned to white persons. ... The thing to accomplish was, under the guise of giving equal accommodation for whites and blacks, to compel the latter to keep to themselves while traveling in railroad passenger coaches. No one would be so wanting in candor as to assert the contrary.

Allowing discrimination by private individuals could be explained as part of the court's commitment to individualism or the federal government's limited role. Discrimination imposed by a state government on businesses (not to mention their customers) that would just as soon not bother was a whole other issue.

The low point came in 1898, when the Supreme Court handed down its opinion in *Williams v. Mississippi*. Technically this was a criminal procedure case; Williams was found guilty of murder but objected to the pool of people that his jury had been drawn from. But because Mississippi's law had the same standards for voting and serving on juries, this was also, in effect, a voting rights case.

Mississippi state law applied a poll tax and literacy test on potential jurors and voters. The reading test was set up to be arbitrary, with local officials in control of testing and no consistent standard of what a passing grade would be. The poll tax presented a burden on poor households. Both had the effect of screening African Americans from voting and serving on juries -- a point the state of Mississippi admitted. The Supreme Court allowed this arrangement to stand unanimously. Even John Marshall Harlan passed on filing a dissent. The decision did not even warn states to administer reading tests and poll taxes fairly.

Southern states in particular would exploit the Williams decision, adding in "grandfather" clauses that would allow exemptions from the reading tests if an ancestor had been a voter. Since virtually all African Americans had been barred from voting before the Civil War, this meant that an illiterate white was probably exempt from the literacy test, while an educated black would have to pass a test that was likely to be rigged against him.

But the Supreme Court was hardly alone in abandoning the Reconstruction Amendments. After the controversial Presidential election of 1876 Democrats dropped objections to the election of Republican Rutherford B. Hayes. In exchange the Hayes administration withdrew occupation troops from the southern states and allowed the Democratic administrations in the south a free hand. Congress did not consider any further civil rights bills, and the Hayes administration put little effort into enforcing those already in place. With political support for equal rights dwindling, the federal courts would have been hard-pressed to enforce the Reconstruction Amendments on their own.

Still, the Supreme Court did find one place to stand, and that was on the "Freedom of Contract." In the 1905 case of *New York v. Lochner*, the court considered a law limiting the number of hours that bakery employees could work -- no more than 10 hours a day and 60 per week.

The bakeries could be dangerous places to work. Heat from the ovens could be stifling. Flour dust damaged lungs. Baking sugar attracted insects. Lochner's bakery was actually one of the better ones. In between preparing dough and inserting it into the ovens Lochner would allow his staff to rest for a few hours in an onsite dormitory. Paying them for the rest period put him over the 60-hour limit, however.

Typically state "police power" included workplace regulations. But the Supreme Court, reluctant to use the Reconstruction Amendments to protect Civil Rights, found a creative application for the 14th Amendment at last.

The First section of the 14th Amendment holds that

> All persons born or naturalized in the United States, and subject to the jurisdiction thereof, are citizens of the United States and of the State wherein they reside. No State shall make or enforce any law

which shall abridge the privileges or immunities of citizens of the United States; *nor shall any State deprive any person of life, liberty, or property, without due process of law*; nor deny to any person within its jurisdiction the equal protection of the laws. (emphasis added)

Rufus Peckham was the son of an attorney from Albany, New York. He learned law on his own, studying in his father's library, and then started his own practice before winning an appointment as a trial court judge and then working his way up to that state's highest court before Grover Cleveland tapped him for the US Supreme Court. As an influential attorney and judge in New York, Peckham was familiar with some of the most powerful men of finance and industry at the time, and the experience may have made him sympathetic to business interests.

Writing for a narrow five-to-four majority, Peckham focused on the "liberty" that states were not to take away under the Fourteenth Amendment without due process of law. The drafters of the amendment clearly had the shackles of slavery foremost in their minds when they wrote those words, but for Peckham that liberty was broader, and included the right to agree to a contract with an employer and work for whatever hours one was willing to work.

This liberty of contract was an essential freedom, and the ordinary process of legislation did not constitute an adequate process of law to take it away. And thus New York could not violate the liberty to work in a bakery for more than 60 hours a week:

The statute necessarily interferes with the right of contract between the employer and employees, concerning the number of hours in which the latter may labor in the bakery of the employer. The general right to make a contract in relation to his business is part of the liberty of the individual protected by the 14th Amendment of the Federal Constitution. ... Under that provision no state can deprive any person of life, liberty, or property without due process of law. The right to purchase or to sell labor is part of the liberty protected by this amendment, unless there are circumstances which exclude the right.

Peckham saw a threat to workers from all this legislative interference.

It is unfortunately true that labor, even in any department, may possibly carry with it the seeds of unhealthiness. But are we all, on that account, at the mercy of legislative majorities? A printer, a tinsmith, a locksmith, a carpenter, a cabinetmaker, a dry goods clerk, a bank's, a lawyer's, or a physician's clerk, or a clerk in almost any kind of business, would all come under the power of the legislature, on this assumption. No trade, no occupation, no mode of earning one's living, could escape this all-pervading power, and the acts of the legislature in limiting the hours of labor in all employments would be valid, although such limitation might seriously cripple the ability of the laborer to support himself and his family.

Justice Harlan dissented, citing research showing that baking was a particularly hazardous occupation and arguing that the court should give some respect to the lawmakers of New York State. But it was a more recent appointee, Oliver Wendell Holmes, who cut to the heart of the matter:

> This case is decided upon an economic theory which a large part of the country does not entertain. If it were a question whether I agreed with that theory, I should desire to study it further and long before making up my mind. But I do not conceive that to be my duty, because I strongly believe that my agreement or disagreement has nothing to do with the right of a majority to embody their opinions in law. It is settled by various decisions of this court that state constitutions and state laws may regulate life in many ways which we as legislators might think as injudicious, or if you like as tyrannical, as this, and which, equally with this, interfere with the liberty to contract. Sunday laws and usury laws are ancient examples. A more modern one is the prohibition of lotteries. The liberty of the citizen to do as he likes so long as he does not interfere with the liberty of others to do the same, which has been a shibboleth for some well-known writers, is interfered with by school laws, by the Post Office, by every state or municipal institution which takes his money for purposes thought desirable, whether he likes it or not.

Some positives did emerge from Fuller's time on the Supreme Court. As the Union grew the caseloads got even more difficult. Fuller lobbied Congress for relief and got it in 1891, when a new Judiciary Act created a Court of Appeals to provide the first review of cases from the federal courts -- which cut back on the Supreme Court's caseload considerably. The Justices were also -- finally -- relieved of all circuit-riding duties.

The changes meant that the Supreme Court could focus on the most pressing issues and give them their full attention, living and working full-time in Washington, DC.

The Fuller Court may have been indecisive on civil rights for African Americans, but they did take a critical step in enforcing civil rights. Originally the Bill of Rights only applied to the Federal government. But in the case of Chicago, Quincy, and Burlington Railroad v. City of Chicago they determined that the Due Process Clause of the 14th Amendment had in effect made the states subject to the Bill of Rights as well.

The details remained to be worked out, and there were some false steps along the way, but on the whole the "incorporation" of the Bill of Rights into the 14th Amendment -- and its application to the states -- increased the freedoms that Americans enjoy today.

CHAPTER FOUR
A Gradual Turn

Edward Douglas White would step into Fuller's role in December 1910. Unlike most Chief Justices, White was promoted from within, having already served 16 years as a Supreme Court Justice.

His credentials as a judge were solid. A native of Louisiana, White had been appointed to that state's highest court and served as a Senator. Before that he had studied law at the University of Louisiana Law School (the forerunner of Tulane) in New Orleans. He had great family connections. His father had served as a Congressman and Governor. The family had a large sugar plantation west of New Orleans with dozens of slaves.

What White had done before studying law was a bit murkier. He appears to have served in the Confederate Army, though which units he served in and what battles he fought in isn't clear. Most likely he was part of a guerilla unit that harassed Union forces occupying Louisiana. By the war's end he had been captured and held as a POW. After the war he was paroled and returned to his family's now abandoned plantation, where he began his legal studies. There were suspicions that he had joined the Ku Klux Klan at one point, though proof was shaky.

Under Edward White, the Supreme Court continued to hold to its belief in the primacy of the right to contract. In theory this might have been meant to liberate both companies and workers. In practice this liberty of contract tended to empower employers, as in the case of "yellow-dog" contracts that prohibited employees from joining unions. In the case of *Coppage v. Kansas*, the Supreme Court acknowledged the imbalance in bargaining power, and then proceeded to strike down a state law that prohibited such contracts anyway. Writing for a seven-member majority, Justice Mahlon Pitney explained that for workers it was just a hard old world sometimes:

> As to the interest of the employed, it is said by the Kansas supreme court to be a matter of common knowledge that 'employees, as a rule, are not financially able to be as independent in making contracts for the sale of their labor as are employers in making a contract of purchase thereof.' No doubt, wherever the right of private property exists, there must and will be inequalities of fortune ... unless all things are held in common, some persons must have more property than others, it is from the nature of things impossible to uphold freedom of contract and

the right of private property without at the same
time recognizing as legitimate those inequalities of
fortune that are the necessary result of the exercise
of those rights.

The White Court did manage to lay down some standards on
civil rights for African Americans. Southern states had
refined their methods for excluding black voters. The poll
taxes and reading tests tripped up some poor and
uneducated whites, so "grandfather" clauses were added to
state laws: if you had an ancestor who was allowed to vote in
the past -- typically some point before the 15th Amendment
and its guarantee of voting rights for blacks -- then you were
exempted from one or more of the other requirements.

The Supreme Court had turned a blind eye toward the ill
intentions behind the reading tests and poll taxes, but the
Grandfather Clause Cases were too blatant. In 1914 White
wrote a decision striking the Grandfather Clause down in
Oklahoma. The victory was purely tactical, however. The
court allowed states to collect poll taxes and apply reading
tests capriciously. It was a first step, but few African
Americans got their ballots back in Oklahoma or anywhere
else the ruling applied.

More valuable was the decision in *Bailey v. Alabama*.
Alabama state law placed a stiff penalty on a worker who
received a cash advance and then failed to complete his
assignment -- he could be subjected to forced labor until the
contract was completed and the advance was paid off.

To make matters worse, under the same law the jury in these cases was to be instructed that failure to complete work was itself proof of intent to defraud. This assumption made it more difficult for defendants to argue that they broke the contract for some other reason -- such as illness, injury, or a family emergency. The contract needed to be in writing, but that didn't preclude trickery against illiterate workers.

The practical effect was Alabama had reinstated peonage, a close relative of slavery, that Alabama workers could fall into and be forced to labor for months or maybe years to pay their way out of.

The Supreme Court made a point of rejecting any claim that Alabama's law was motivated by racism: "We at once dismiss from consideration that the plaintiff...is a black man" wrote Justice Hughes, who continued "... the statute on its face makes no racial discrimination, and the record fails to show its existence in fact. No question of a sectional character is presented, and we may view the legislation in the same manner as if it had been enacted in New York or in Idaho."

Nonetheless, the court found by a seven-to-two majority that the 13th Amendment's prohibition on forced servitude applied, and that it made the Alabama statute void. It was another small step, but they were steps in the right direction. The Supreme Court was beginning to apply the Reconstruction Amendments as they were meant to be applied.

White was succeeded as Chief Justice by former President William Howard Taft. Like White, Taft was a conservative leader of a conservative court, but it was a conservatism that had a measure of respect for the Constitution and the intentions of those who wrote it.

Taft grew up near Cincinnati, Ohio, in a family that was well-off though not fabulously wealthy. His father had been a diplomat and a judge, and was one of the founders of the Skull and Bones secret society at Yale. William followed in his footsteps, attending Yale and studying law at the University of Cincinnati.

A promising legal career took a detour when Taft was named the head of a commission to oversee the creation of a civilian government in the Philippines. While there Taft made a point of treating the Filipinos as social equals, though he felt that establishing a democratic republic there would be long-term project. His term there was considered successful enough that he became the Republican nominee for President in 1908 and was elected. But he only served one term in the White House. After that, he began his pursuit of the role he coveted most: Supreme Court Justice.

Taft enjoyed the cut and thrust of legal argument -- perhaps a bit too much, as debates among justices could get to be feisty at times. But he was a great advocate for the court itself.

One can fairly say that the Supreme Court as we know it today emerged during Taft's term as Chief Justice. He lobbied Congress for legislation that increased the Supreme Court's supervision of the Courts of Appeal. This improved coordination between the two levels of the federal judiciary, so federal judges were more likely to be on the same page. The system of Writs of Certiorari emerged at the same time: From Taft's time on the Supreme Court would get to choose the cases it felt were most important.

Finally, Taft pushed for the Supreme Court to get its own office building and courtroom, outside of the Capitol Building. The Supreme Court was allotted a city block's worth of land, across First Street from the Capitol. Taft hired a friend, Cass Gilbert, to design the structure. It would turn out to be a grand, even lavish building, befitting a court of great stature. But Chief Justice Taft would not live to see it built.

For the most part the Supreme Court under Taft followed its older precedents. But the court made some modest changes to the law, and most were positive. Perhaps the most important was its decision to incorporate more of the Bill of Rights under the 14th Amendment -- assuring that civil rights were protected from abuse by both the federal government and the states. One of the most important decisions was *Gitlow v. New York*.

Benjamin Gitlow was, to be quite frank, a communist. As the business manager of the New York-based Revolutionary Age, he published a "Left-Wing manifesto" that began:

> "The world is in crisis. Capitalism, the prevailing system of society, is in process of disintegration and collapse. Out of its vitals is developing a new social order, the system of Communist Socialism; and the struggle between this new social order and the old,

is now the fundamental problem of international politics."

And from there the manifesto went on to call for a revolution that would smash both capitalism and democracy in order to establish a "proletarian dictatorship" under the guidance of the Communist International. It was radical stuff to be sure. But was it illegal? The State of New York found that it was and sentenced Gitlow to 5-10 years at Sing-Sing Prison for "Criminal Anarchy."

Gitlow appealed to the Supreme Court, which upheld the conviction, but along the way it determined that New York was obligated to respect free speech rights. This was a major change; originally the First Amendment only applied to the federal government.

Gitlow was left to serve out his sentence because the court found that his "manifesto" promoted violence. It wasn't a theoretical piece about the merits of socialism or the eventual fate of American capitalism; the manifesto called for the eventual overthrow of the American system of government. Even if the manifesto implied that the Revolution was still several years away, under New York's law that was illegal and the Supreme Court let that stand for the time being.

But it was a close call. Justices Louis Brandeis and Oliver Wendell Holmes dissented, arguing that even radical speech like the "Left-Wing Manifesto" should be protected unless it called for violent acts in the near term. Eventually the Supreme Court would bolster the protection of speech at all levels of government. But after *Gitlow* state lawmakers were at least on notice that the courts would be watching how they treated people who held unpopular opinions.

Until 1923 the federal courts had been very lenient with the conduct of state criminal trials. If the state's appellate courts were satisfied that the defendant had a fair trial with an impartial judge and jury the federal courts would not intervene. That changed with the case of *Moore v. Dempsey*.

The case started after a race riot in rural eastern Arkansas that led to the death of five whites and an unknown number of African Americans -- estimates of black deaths run from 25 to nearly a thousand. After the riot was quelled, a local grand jury indicted 12 black "ringleaders," accusing them of the murder of a white man amid the mayhem.

Oliver Wendell Holmes described what happened next as part of the court's decision:

> ...the petitioners were brought into court, informed that a certain lawyer was appointed their counsel, and were placed on trial before a white jury -- blacks being systematically excluded from both grand and petit juries. The court and neighborhood were thronged with an adverse crowd that threatened the most dangerous consequences to anyone interfering with the desired result. The counsel did not venture to demand delay or a change of venue, to challenge a juryman or to ask for separate trials. He had had no preliminary consultation with the accused, called no witnesses for the defense, although they could have

been produced, and did not put the defendants on the stand. The trial lasted about three-quarters of an hour, and in less than five minutes, the jury brought in a verdict of guilty of murder in the first degree. According to the allegations and affidavits, there never was a chance for the petitioners to be acquitted; no juryman could have voted for an acquittal and continued to live in Phillips County, and if any prisoner by any chance had been acquitted by a jury, he could not have escaped the mob.

The defendants were sentenced to death. After the Arkansas courts upheld the verdict, the defendants requested a Writ of Habeus Corpus from the federal court, which was turned down. They then appealed to the Supreme Court, which took up the case. During argument the attorney representing the State acknowledged that there was a large and unruly crowd at the courthouse, and that the trial and jury deliberations were unusually short given the stakes. The state's argument rested on the fact that there had been a trial, and an appeal in the state courts, that the legal forms were followed, and that the state courts were satisfied with the overall procedure.

Holmes, with the support of five fellow justices, wasn't having any of it:

> ...if the case is that the whole proceeding is a mask -- that counsel, jury and judge were swept to the fatal end by an irresistible wave of public passion, and that the State Courts failed to correct the wrong;

neither perfection in the machinery for correction nor the possibility that the trial court and counsel saw no other way of avoiding an immediate outbreak of the mob can prevent this court from securing to the petitioners their constitutional rights.

Holmes and his fellow justices professed to be undecided on the guilt or innocence of the defendants. Rather than set the defendants free they sent the case back to the federal court for further hearings. But Arkansas politicians and judges got the hint: within a year all 12 of the supposed "ringleaders" were released, either by court order or executive pardon.

Most important, there would be no more automatic acceptance of state criminal trials. Federal court judges were expected to investigate and rule on bias accusations and grant Habeus Corpus relief where they found significant violations of constitutional rights. When the Warren Court revamped criminal procedural law in the 1960s, much of it was built on the foundation that Oliver Wendell Holmes laid here.

In 1929 the United States entered a severe period of economic stagnation that would be known as The Great Depression. The American economy had hit rough patches before, but those had been relatively mild, short-lived, or both. The Great

Depression would stand out for its severity and duration. At its worst a quarter of the workforce would be unemployed. Median income of American households would drop by half. The Depression called into question the laissez-faire economic theories that stood behind the court's liberty of contract doctrines. The imbalance of bargaining power between employers and employees, waved off a few years ago, began to loom larger.

Chief Justice Taft's health began fading at about the same time, and he resigned in February 1930, just as the depth of the Great Depression was manifesting itself. President Herbert Hoover selected Charles Evans Hughes.

CHAPTER FIVE
A Switch in Time

Remarkably, this was not Charles Evans Hughes' first stint on the Supreme Court. The New Yorker had served as an Associate Justice from 1910 to 1916, where he had shown himself to be a moderate progressive. He sided with the majority in the *Bailey v. Alabama* decision that struck down peonage, and also voted to strike down grandfather clauses. His judicial philosophy was close to that of Oliver Wendell Holmes.

Hughes was as much a politician as a judge. He quit the court in 1916 to run for President, losing the general election to Woodrow Wilson. After that he served as Secretary of State for Warren Harding. Later on he was appointed to the Permanent Court of International Justice.

Shortly after Hughes took over as Chief Justice, work began on the Supreme Court Building that Taft had envisioned. It was a lavish building that would come to be known as "The Marble Palace." Each Justice had office space and access to a full legal library on site. Chief Justice Hughes and his successors would hold an exalted place in the center chair at the front of the grandest courtroom in the nation, if not the whole world.

The Supreme Court continued to move slowly but steadily on civil rights. Two cases -- one notorious, the other somewhat obscure, show the court's evolution. The notorious case was that of the "Scottsboro Boys," a convoluted story involving nine young black males ranging in age from 19 to 13. After sneaking onto a freight train going through Alabama, hoping to find work in the next town, they got into a fight with some whites who had also snuck onto the same train. Just as they were captured at a stop just outside of Scottsboro, two white women also emerged from the train and accused the nine blacks of raping them.

What followed was a decades-long saga of trials -- before all-white juries -- and appeals that went up to the Supreme Court twice. Both times the court set aside convictions. The second time, in the 1935 case of *Norris v. Alabama*, the Supreme Court determined that African Americans must be given a fair chance to serve on juries. It was a significant break from prior decisions because the court looked at overall patterns and practices. A law that didn't mention race overtly could still violate equal protection.

The less famous case involved the notion of "separate but equal." Lloyd Gaines, an aspiring black attorney from Saint Louis, wanted to attend the University of Missouri's law school. His grades were good enough, but Missouri did not allow black students, and none of the other law schools in the state accepted African Americans either. The State of Missouri offered to pay Gaines tuition at an out-of-state school, but this was not acceptable to Gaines, who was represented by Thurgood Marshall of the National Association for the Advancement of Colored People.

Chief Justice Hughes, writing for a six-to-two majority, agreed, up to a point:

> The basic consideration is not as to what sort of opportunities other States provide, or whether they are as good as those in Missouri, but as to what opportunities Missouri itself furnishes to white students and denies to negroes solely upon the ground of color. The admissibility of laws separating the races in the enjoyment of privileges afforded by the State rests wholly upon the equality

of the privileges which the laws give to the separated groups within the State. ...The white resident is afforded legal education within the State, the negro resident having the same qualifications is refused it there and must go outside the State to obtain it. That is a denial of the equality of legal right to the enjoyment of the privilege which the State has set up, and the provision for the payment of tuition fees in another State does not remove the discrimination.

Hughes concluded that Gaines "was entitled to be admitted to the law school of the State University *in the absence of other and proper provision for his legal training within the State.*" (emphasis added) The State of Missouri latched onto that, creating a law school for African Americans at the state's black college, Lincoln University in Saint Louis. The Supreme Court was determined that "separate but equal" should mean something; that it shouldn't be a license for states to neglect the interests of African American citizens. But they weren't ready to establish outright integration as the norm across the country.

The NAACP was eager to challenge the sufficiency of this hastily thrown-together law school for blacks, but Lloyd Gaines suddenly disappeared. To this day his whereabouts remain unknown. He might have been murdered by whites who resented his lawsuit. Or he might have had enough of the attention and pressure that comes with being a litigant in a federal lawsuit. Thurgood Marshall, however, would become a fixture as a lawyer before the Supreme Court, eventually joining it as a Justice.

Ordinarily Chief Justices still sought to minimize dissension on the court, but that proved impossible in the 1930s. The division among justices became sharpest on economic issues and the "liberty of contract." As Franklin Delano Roosevelt entered the White House, there was a clear division between progressives and conservatives. On the left were the "Three Musketeers": Louis Brandeis, Benjamin Cardozo, and Harlan Stone. On the right were "The Four Horsemen": Pierce Butler, James Clark, McReynolds, George Sutherland, and Willis Van Devanter. That left two in the middle: Chief Justice Hughes and the newest Associate, Owen Roberts.

At first the conservatives authored most of the decisions; with their extra vote they only needed to persuade one of the two swing Justices. But their grip was less than total. The Roosevelt administration and many states responded to the Depression with tighter marketplace regulations. Many of these new rules threatened the liberty of contract that the court had established in the Lochner decision.

The Hughes Court did allow the states some more leeway than they had in the past. Among the many effects of the Depression was a sharp drop in farm prices -- milk, grain, meat, eggs, and the like. The State of New York passed legislation setting a minimum price for milk, and the Supreme Court let it stand in a decision that raised a few eyebrows. Prior decisions had set parallels between wages and commodity prices -- a wage is a price after all -- and allowing government to set limits on one implied they could set limits on the other, despite the earlier ruling in *Lochner*.

The court also gave its approval to regulations of fees that insurance companies could pay their agents in New Jersey, and a Minnesota moratorium on farm foreclosures -- all of which chipped away at liberty of contract.

But the Supreme Court still disapproved of interference from the federal Congress. The Roosevelt Administration was taking maximum advantage of a Democratic majority in both houses of Congress to pass aggressive, even radical legislation.

 Among the most controversial was the National Industrial Recovery Act (NIRA) of 1933. NIRA allowed industry and labor representatives to agree on "codes of fair competition," including standards for wages, hours, and working conditions. The President could then adopt these codes, giving them the force of law.

Ordinarily, the responsibility for enacting federal laws fell upon Congress. In prior years the Supreme Court had allowed the executive branch to make and enforce rules on its own, but only with the authorization of Congress, which was expected to provide guidelines. Federal courts kept a close eye on this process by which Congress "delegated" its lawmaking authority to the President.

The National Industrial Recovery Act was delegation run amok. Lawmaking power essentially went from Congress through the President on down to private groups. And the act gave little guidance about the goals and methods that management and labor representatives were to pursue as they legislated rules for their own industries. That was an awful lot of power to put in the hands of private groups, with no guarantee that the executive branch would provide enough supervision.

Franklin Roosevelt had made the National Industrial Relations Act and its industrial codes a high priority, so there was a great deal of excitement when the Supreme Court agreed to hear the case of *ALA. Schechter Poultry Corp. v. United States.*

The Schechter Brothers operated a kosher slaughterhouse and retail poultry store in New York City. The Roosevelt administration had approved a Code of Fair Competition for the New York area, and the Schechters were accused of 18 violations. One involved the selling of an unfit chicken -- the newspapers took to calling it the "sick chicken case" -- but most were for allowing customers to select a chicken before it was butchered, a no-no under the code.

The result was a different kind of slaughter. The court decided, unanimously, that the process of creating these fair competition codes violated the Constitution. Congress couldn't turn over its authority all at once like this. In addition, because the codes were often local in nature -- like the one that tripped up the Schechters -- The National Industrial Recovery Act interfered with local commerce, which was supposed to be left to the states.

The Supreme Court also struck down the Agricultural Adjustment Act, in which the federal government sought to reduce production of meat, grains, and produce in order to boost prices. It did the same with the Bituminous Coal Act, which set the price for that critical fuel.

Incensed, President Roosevelt railed against the "Nine Old Men" who blocked his plan to give Americans relief from the Depression. The age issue resonated with the public, and sensing his opportunity Roosevelt and his supporters in Congress proposed an increase in the size of the court, adding one justice for every sitting justice over the age of 70.

This court-packing plan became the center of heated debate. On the one hand, Roosevelt's economic program, the "New Deal," was immensely popular with the public. Roosevelt won a thumping victory for re-election in 1936, taking 61 percent of the vote and all but two states. But dramatically changing the Supreme Court's makeup to preserve Roosevelt's program struck many as setting a dangerous precedent. Public opinion supported Roosevelt over the Nine Old Men at first but gradually shifted away from his Supreme Court "reform" plan.

Court packing became a moot issue in 1937 when Owen Morris started siding with the liberal bloc. The first sign of the shift came in *West Coast Hotel v. Parrish*, which upheld a Washington state minimum wage law. From there the Supreme Court began finding more ways to uphold economic regulations. Exceptions to Liberty of Contract meant the slow death of the Lochner decision. In *NLRB v. Jones and Laughlin Steel*, the Supreme Court developed the notion of the "stream of commerce" -- and allowed Congress to regulate anything likely to affect that stream as a part of "interstate commerce."

The court wasn't about to revive the old National Industrial Recovery Act -- Congress wouldn't be allowed to delegate lawmaking to private companies or unions, and the NIRA was a hastily drafted mess anyway -- but anything short of that was in play. Congress and the President now had more power to regulate businesses, establish wage and hour standards, promote collective bargaining, and set agricultural prices.

Over time, Franklin Roosevelt got the court he wanted, and he got it the old-fashioned way: winning elections and making his own appointments as the older Justices retired. By 1945, when Roosevelt passed away, eight of the nine were his appointees.

In the summer of 1941, the Second World War was raging in Europe and eastern Asia. America was still at peace, though it would only be a few months before it was drawn into the fighting. Charles Evans Hughes, aged 79, realized that he would not be able to continue the work of leading the Supreme Court much longer, and handed in his resignation. President Roosevelt chose to elevate Harlan Fiske Stone, an Associate Justice for 16 years, to Chief Justice.

www.ingramcontent.com/pod-product-compliance
Lightning Source LLC
Chambersburg PA
CBHW070501220526
45466CB00004B/1923